MY TINY

INDOOR
GARDEN

MY TINY

INDOOR GARDEN

BIG IDEAS FOR SMALL SPACES

LIA LEENDERTZ

PAVILION

First published in paperback in the United Kingdom in 2018 by
Pavilion Books Company Limited
43 Great Ormond Street
London WC1N 3HZ

ISBN 978-1-911624-19-6

A CIP catalogue record for this book is available from the British Library.

10 9 8 7 6 5 4 3 2 1

Reproduction by Mission Productions Ltd, Hong Kong
Printed and bound by Toppan Leefung Printing Ltd, China

This book can be ordered direct from the publisher at www.pavilionbooks.com

CONTENTS

INTRODUCTION

There is nothing lovelier than gazing upon greenery; it rests the eyes and soothes the soul. It does this just as well indoors as out. Put a group of houseplants in the corner of a room and that room comes alive; you feel you can really breathe fresh air when there are plants around you.

Indoor plants have never gone away, but they are currently enjoying a particularly enthusiastic revival among city-dwellers and those living in temporary or small accommodation, with little or no outdoor space. It's perfectly logical: if you have a home that you cannot make any permanent changes to, you can personalise it by filling its windowsills and alcoves with your own plants. When you have to move, you can pack up your little indoor garden in a box and take it with you to make your next house feel instantly like your home. If you don't have floor space you can fit indoor plants along shelves, or even hang them in baskets from walls or ceilings. There is no home so small and so short-term that you cannot create an indoor garden within it.

Houseplants have a wonderful presence and they win out over pieces of art and even the best-loved furniture because they change over time. The pony-tail palm cared for since it was bought for small change at a flea market, the aspidistra passed on by a grandfather which has seen out two world wars and the cheese plant bought to cheer up a first bedsit which now looms, triffid-like, from a corner – we become attached to these plants because they have lived, breathed and grown alongside us. And they don't have to be tricky; there is a houseplant for everyone, from the slow-growing and undemanding cacti and succulents to the high-maintenance green and glossy tropical plants. Indoor plants will keep your green fingers occupied all winter if you are a gardener longing for spring, but if their decorative value is your main interest they will simply sit prettily on your mantelpiece asking for nothing but the occasional dusting.

Within this book there are examples of many types of indoor garden – some colourful, some green, some demanding, some easy. All of them enhance the homes and lives of the people who care for them. If you have ever considered starting your own tiny indoor garden, you will find all the inspiration you need from these indoor gardeners.

'I grow plants for many reasons:
to please my eye or to please my soul, to
challenge the elements or to challenge
my patience, for novelty or for nostalgia,
but mostly for the joy in seeing them grow.'

David Hobson

Little succulents (far left) contain a world of colours and textures.

Create a tropical, leafy atmosphere in your home using big green houseplants.

9

BRINGING THE OUTSIDE IN

When we think of houseplants, a certain set of plants comes to mind: they are generally green, lush and tropical in look and feel. But some gardeners prefer to look closer to home for their indoor plants and create displays that have more in common with miniature gardens, or with tiny corners of woodland, than they do with any jungle. These gardeners are turning to the outdoors and finding ways to bring it indoors: as flowering bulb displays, in tiny verdant terrariums of fern and moss, or just as garden plants potted up and arranged so that their delicate natural beauty can be truly appreciated.

A rainbow of antique glass vases is arrayed across Jeroen's windowsill, each filled with a deliciously scented, pure white-flowered hyacinth.

A RAINBOW OF VASES

'I am an eBay obsessive,' says Jeroen Bergmans, and in the kitchen of his London flat the spoils are all around him: bright red 1960s Danish cooking pots; a wall of Victorian fern prints; 1950s furniture and lamps. The beautiful collection of hyacinth vases filling his kitchen windowsill comes mainly from the same source, and from the same magpie instinct.

Jeroen has a strong design aesthetic and his love of modern furniture is evident throughout his London flat. 'I like to fill a space and make a statement,' he says. 'I wasn't particularly interested in growing a few hyacinths here and there around the place; I wanted to create a feature that would become a part of the architecture of the house.'

The first vase, a chunky 1950s piece in salmon-coloured glass, was a present from his father. 'I loved the shape and colour of it, so I started looking out for more,' says Jeroen. He was first inspired in his choice of colour by a table he had coveted when working on an interiors magazine. 'At first I bought shades of amber, and then I added greens and pinks. I wanted a simple and muted palette of colours, and I prefer them arranged within their colours like a rainbow, rather than all jumbled up. It makes more of an impact.'

Jeroen is originally from Amsterdam. The Dutch are famous for their love of bulbs, of course, but they also have a great passion for houseplants. 'No one in Amsterdam has curtains,' says Jeroen. 'Everyone's windows are filled with houseplants instead, so it seems quite natural to me that my front window should be filled with growing plants.' His 30 jostling hyacinth spires create a visual barrier between the kitchen and the road, and are prettier – and certainly more fragrant – than a pair of net curtains.

Hyacinth vases are designed to hold the plant so that the bulb is just above the water to avoid it rotting, but the roots can easily trail down into the water, drinking it up and watering the bulb as it stretches into flower. The vases achieve this by means of a wide base, a wide top and a cinched-in waist, but Jeroen's collection shows just how many possible ways these particular dice can fall. Some of the vases are squat and plump, luxuriantly hourglass in shape, some are tall and elegant like an Empire-line dress, while still others are decidedly pear-shaped; some are wavy-topped and others ribbed, some sleek and modern, others hookah-like. What all have in common is that they hold the bulb exactly where it needs to be, just above the water, and they make almost as much of a feature of the roots, twisting and spreading in the water, as they do of the flowers themselves.

Although it would be possible for him to force hyacinths from chilled bulbs, Jeroen prefers the more fail-safe route of buying them as plants when they are just ready to flower. 'I have bought and grown them as bulbs before but it is a tricky job and lots of them failed. Now I buy them at Columbia Road Flower Market, where they are sold grown on in soil. I carefully wash the soil off the roots and feed the roots into the base of the vase.' He always chooses white-flowered bulbs: 'I don't want any colours that are going to clash with the colours of the vases, and it is important to me that they all look the same.'

*With a great interest in interior design, Jeroen has
collected antique Delft tiles, old trunks and 1960s
furniture. Plants and collections are carefully placed
together to show each off to its best.*

The first of Jeroen's hyacinth vases was a pale, salmon-pink vase with a complicated, faceted surface, a gift from his father. It set him on the path to his current beautiful collection, all from different eras and in different shapes, but in similar dusky hues.

In Amsterdam, where Jeroen grew up, people very rarely hang net curtains and instead fill their windows with houseplants. Jeroen wanted to do the same in his London flat.

17

SHELFIES

'I find houseplants too static on their own,' says designer and stylist **Amanda Russell of her shelf collection of houseplants, outdoor plants, cut flowers and pretty things. 'I like the fluidity that plants from the garden bring – they flower for a short time before they fade and I replace them with something else. It keeps the display fresh and interesting.'**

Amanda has her own business, R & B Designs, with fellow designer Juliet Bawden. Her day job involves styling for magazine shoots and creating 'makes' for craft magazines – taking standard ceramics and giving them textures, marbling book covers, or giving a paint effect to a bench. You would think that this would prove enough of a channel for her creativity, but it seems not. 'I just love to create little scenes,' she says. 'I have always been attracted by museums and botanical specimens and I think I am trying to create a sort of Victorian scientific display, my own natural history museum. I fill tiny bottles with single stems and I find I appreciate the flowers more when they are singled out in this way.'

One of the hellebore flowers from Amanda's garden joins the display on her plant-filled shelves.

Amanda has always loved plants and once took on an allotment, but she found that the time and commitment it required were too much to fit into a busy life. 'With indoor plants they are just there, and you can fiddle with them as you go about the house,' she says. She has a set of pure white shelves that are well lit by a nearby window and uses this for her main houseplant display. While she likes using ferns such as her Boston and maidenhair ferns as they blend well with the elements that come in from the garden, Amanda is unsentimental about replacing them. 'I look after them, but I like them looking good. I treat plants much like a bunch of flowers.' She feels the same about the outdoor plants that she brings in temporarily. 'I do plant them back out afterwards but sometimes they don't like the transition. That's all right – I can buy something else nice when I see it.' An example of this approach is a newly bought tray of little white and blue-faced pansies transferred into terracotta pots and nestling happily among longer-term residents.

As with the plants, Amanda has a constantly revolving stream of beautiful props coming into the house and jostling for space on her shelf. 'I am a stylist so I spend a lot of time at flea markets, buying and selling: you have to circulate your junk.' She once had her stall cleared out as soon as she arrived. 'The man was saying, "This is all gorgeous! I'll take the lot!" I asked him what he wanted it for and he said he was a stylist. I didn't have the heart to tell him the stuff had already done the rounds.' She loves lettering, and particularly enjoys the juxtaposition of the elegant and straightforward writing on her antique jars. Her beautiful piece of white coral is a long-term fixture.

Amanda's garden is a great source for pretty clippings and cuttings. 'I love to pluck little things from the garden and put them into glass jars, or my big test tube – I suspend that against the wall using Command hooks, which you can move about. I am one of the few gardeners who is really enthusiastic about pruning as it gives me lots of new material.' The result is an eclectic composition that is constantly fresh and intriguing.

Amanda loves to combine finds from jumble sales and charity shops with houseplants and flowers from the garden. She uses white containers and objets against a white wall and then fills the containers with a variety of textures and colours in the form of leaves and flowers.

An orchid from a garden centre and a set of pansies from her garden look equally at home on Amanda's set of shelves.

Amanda works as a stylist and one of her favourite tricks is to suspend test tube-style containers and place single stems in them.

Amanda likes to put flowers from the garden, such as blossom, dead nettle and leucojum among her houseplants.

Terrariums are ecosystems in miniature – beautiful little worlds of compost, gravel, plants and moss.

A WORLD IN A BOTTLE

In her studio in east London, Emma Sibley is in the process of making 150 bottle terrariums, selecting tiny plants from her shelves and teasing them into little portions of compost and gravel. 'These are the smallest I have ever made and I am keen to see how well they work. I always make them a couple of weeks before they are needed so that they have time to settle in,' she says.

These lovely little objects were ordered by a company keen to give them out to journalists on a press day, indicative of the way her terrariums have caught imaginations. 'It all started when a friend and I made one in the kitchen,' she says. 'Once you've made a terrarium you think "Ooh, I could do that differently." It becomes slightly addictive.' Another friend opened a café and asked Emma for a few terrariums to decorate it, and soon people started asking if they could buy them. It wasn't long before shops followed suit, including Heal's, where Emma still works part time as a digital designer. Next she started holding workshops and the business was up and running. 'I haven't had to shout about them at all, they just took off. I've never had to go out of my way to push them, people just seem to find me.' Everyone loves these tiny worlds of plants.

Any glass container can be used to house a terrarium, and Emma makes use of preserving jars, scientific boiling vessels and anything else she can find.

Emma has improvised various tools to help her access the interior of the terrariums, including brushes, corks on sticks and a sweetcorn skewer for picking up any dropped objects.

'I never thought I was a perfectionist until I started making terrariums,' says Emma. But she has amassed a marvellous array of quirky objects to help her get the terrariums just right· spoons lashed to pieces of bamboo to help with positioning compost, brushes intended for painting the wall behind radiators to clean up the glass, corks on sticks to tamp down compost – even an elongated corn on the cob skewer for collecting accidentally dropped corks. Tracking down the containers is also quite a task in itself. 'I look everywhere for them – eBay, charity shops and antiques fairs in particular. I use carboys, pickle jars, demijohns, really whatever I can find. I also love to use scientific boiling vessels.' These are round at the base, so she has commissioned a friend to make cast concrete bases on which they can balance.

And she has slowly gathered a set of plants that work reliably well in the enclosed, humid spaces of a glass bottle garden, chief among which are miniature asparagus ferns, kentia palms, *Ficus pumila* and trailing ivy, all bought as tiny plants to be most easily slotted into the terrariums. She likes to top the surface of each with stones and moss, as they help to seal in moisture while at the same time making the terrarium appear instantly mature, as if they were perfect little portions of forest floor. 'Moss gives a wonderful look, but it is like buttered toast,' she says, 'It always lands the wrong way up.'

Emma mists each terrarium thoroughly once it is made and then seals it with a cork. From then on it should need no other care. A period of two weeks is long enough for her to see that a terrarium has established successfully and she may occasionally have to mist again during this time or replace a plant that has not done well. Generally, though, the humidity in the bottle and the care that Emma takes in planting means that there are no problems. 'There must be no mould. If you open up a terrarium and sniff it the smell should be green and fresh,' she says. 'The aim is always to create a fully functioning, self-sustaining little ecosystem, captured in a beautiful bottle.'

Emma's workshop is filled with the paraphernalia of terrarium-making, from compost and stones to stacks of moss and shelves full of tiny plants. It is the hub of a fast-growing terrarium empire.

HOW TO: TERRARIUMS

A terrarium can be made in any glass container with a lid, though the larger the container, the easier the assembly and the more likely you are to be successful. Once planted and closed up, terrariums should make completely self-sufficient little worlds and should need no further attention, save for gazing into their green depths.

1. Choose your container and fill the base with a layer of gravel or pebbles, washed first to get rid of any dust. Terrariums with obvious layers look great, so make your base layer reasonably thick.

2. Add a teaspoon of activated charcoal powder, which helps to keep away bacteria and prevent the terrarium from turning mouldy. On top of this, add a layer of compost and tamp it down using a stick with a cork on the end or similar. As before, make it a thick layer.

3. Use a stick to make a hole where you want your first plant to go. Brush the compost from the plant and drop it in, then use sticks to manoeuvre it into place and to firmly plant the roots in the soil. Do this with several other plants.

4. Add gravel and moss to the surface to give the terrarium a more 'aged' look, then spray the whole surface with water a good few times, until you can see a rim of darker compost all the way around the edge. Seal with a lid and watch for a week or so, spraying again if you need to. After two weeks it should be settled and no longer in need of any water.

When plants in her garden come into flower, such as these primroses, Emma Bradshaw digs them up and plants them into pretty and unusual containers.

Emma much prefers the look of vegetable seedlings and bulbs to traditional houseplants, and she brings them into the house when they are looking good.

OLD TRADITIONS, MODERN TREASURES

Emma Bradshaw fills her Cotswolds house with greenery, but she has very few traditional houseplants. 'I've never been hugely inspired by houseplants, but I am very fond of wild flowers, and the flowers that grow in my garden,' she says. 'I think they are lovely in the house. They are so much more delicate, more beautiful.'

Emma raids her garden for her favoured plants, carefully digs them up, taking as much root as possible, then pots them and brings them into the house where she can enjoy them up close. 'I particularly love snowdrops, and I have big clumps of them in the garden. I always bring in plenty. Later on there are hellebores and then bluebells. They are always changing – so much more interesting than evergreen plants. I like creating beautiful little corners, little pictures, and these are my favourite plants to use.'

As Emma works for the Gloucestershire Wildlife Trust, it's no surprise that her leanings are towards those plants that grow all around her. 'I always prefer something native. Flowers that I find in the garden are so much better than cut flowers that have been flown in.' Her containers are as unusual as her approach to houseplants: primroses in golden syrup cans, carrot seedlings in a tiny trophy, and alpine primulas in an old bread tin.

Emma works for the local wildlife trust and loves the outdoors, so she is interested in ways that she can bring a little of the wild into her home.

She is as keen on vegetable plants as she is on wild flowers, for practical reasons as well as aesthetic. 'It is quite cold in the garden here, so I put plants out very late. I like to plant them in such a way that I can enjoy them indoors as they grow.' So she has a beautiful packing crate she bought from Stroud market, filled with compost and planted up with tomato seedlings, and an enamel bowl of compost that sprouts feathery carrot tops. She positions them near to windows where possible and away from radiators. Later on they will be planted out and replaced inside with small strawberry plants, alongside stems of cow parsley and twigs of apple blossom. Emma says, 'Creating these things makes me take time to notice the seasons, the passing of winter and the beginning of spring. It is good for my own health and well-being.'

Emma loves to create pretty little corners around her home, using books, plants and other objects she has found.

Carrot seedlings and an alpine primula are planted into containers improvised from kitchen equipment.

*A small forest floor
of bluebells decorates
Emma's plate rack.*

In addition to her work at the Wildlife Trust, Emma also maintains a beautiful blog, Bradshaw & Sons, in which she documents her outdoor life with her three young boys. 'I work at the Trust as Head of Communications, which means that I spend a lot of time writing about wildlife but not a great deal of time actually with it. I decided to make myself get out on adventures with the boys whenever we could.' As well as her trips out and about she uses the blog to document the little still lifes that she creates around the house with her flowers, plants, old books and other collections. 'We collect snail shells and fossils, feathers and stones. It is like an old-fashioned school nature table,' she says. 'I think that is what I am trying to re-create. Our finds end up covering every spare surface.' She loves the reactions of the blogging community to her wildlife posts. 'Early in the year you get a sense of spring rippling up through the country. If I write about bluebells I'll get replies from Scotland saying "Bluebells? What bluebells?"'

Once her indoor garden flowers have faded she puts the plants outside again. 'Sometimes they come back, with a little watering and care. But there are always enough snowdrops and bluebells for me to do the same again next year.'

Containers are unusual and varied: a bark-covered pot for a garden hellebore and an old vegetable crate for tomato seedlings.

Amanda tried her hand at kokedama because she loves to create a magical atmosphere for special dinners or events.

A LITTLE BIT OF MAGIC

Kokedama is the Japanese practice of wrapping a plant's roots in a tight moss ball for display, and it is another of designer Amanda Russell's favourite ways of displaying plants. 'I love the surprise element of it,' she says. 'It is so unexpected. It makes people laugh. I like having flowers on the table but I like having them suspended in little moss balls over the table even more.'

Amanda is generally content to have a bowl of flowering bulbs or a vase of flowers on her dining table, but when there is a special occasion coming up she turns to the theatricality of kokedama. 'This is something I would create for an Easter gathering, or for a pop-up supperclub – an occasion when I want to create some atmosphere and a little bit of magic, something beyond the everyday.' She had been aware of kokedama for some time when she came across a course at nearby Petersham Nurseries in Richmond, Surrey, and signed herself up. 'I was desperate to try it out; it seemed like a Japanese secret art. Little did I know there is very little mystery to it at all.'

Using small flowering bulbs, such as Amanda's scented jonquils and muscari is perhaps the simplest way of creating kokedama, because the bulbs provide most of the nutrients required by the flowers and leaves and there is no need for extra compost to sustain them. However, Amanda has also created kokedamas with perennials from the garden, which is a little more complex. She starts by removing most of the compost from around the roots, then makes a ball using some clay soil. You can source a kokedama soil called akadama from specialist shops online, but if you have a clay garden soil then this will also do the job. She splits the ball in half and sandwiches it around the roots before wrapping it securely in the moss. All types of kokedamas will need a little watering, but perennials will take far more than bulbs, which can get by with the occasional light misting. Perennials will need to be completely dunked in water occasionally.

Traditionally, kokedamas were displayed on small platforms, but the man credited with bringing the craze to the West – Fedor van der Valk, of the Netherlands – had the idea of suspending them and called them 'string gardens'. It is this way of growing them that has caught on, and that Amanda so loves. Van der Valk makes his with tree seedlings and seeds the moss balls with grasses to create little hanging meadows. Others use more traditional houseplants and small ivy plants. 'You can really use any plant you like,' says Amanda, 'but remember that this is a temporary display. After a few days my bulbs will start to look less fresh and I will cut them down and dunk them in some water, then perhaps display them on a platter on the table. Perennials will last longer, but all will fade after a while.' Amanda suspends her kokedamas on fishing wire from a small ladder that she has suspended from the ceiling over the dining table especially for the job, but at other times she has hung them from batons attached to the wall.

She has plans to try this again with tiny strawberry plants, with herbs ('Chives in flower would be wonderful') and with little wild tulips. 'When you encase them in moss and hang them it makes them into a little treasure; you really look at the individual plant. I find myself marvelling at the way the muscari buds are arranged and the way the petals fit together. They become separate specimens rather than a blur of colour, and the flowers and the moss balls really reward such close inspection.'

The roots of houseplants and outdoor plants including small flowering bulbs are trimmed and then wrapped tightly in compost and moss before being hung from a frame. Bulbs are easiest as they do not need compost.

HOW TO: KOKEDAMA

Kokedama is the Japanese art of wrapping the roots of
plants in moss. You can use houseplants or perennials if
you wish, but the technique is perhaps at its simplest with
small flowering bulbs.

1. Select a single bulb that is just coming into flower. Pull it apart from its neighbours, brush most of the soil from the roots, then trim the roots to about 2.5cm (1in) long (7.5cm/3in for perennials and houseplants).

2. Take a piece of moss and spread it out flat on a table as evenly as you can, making sure you have enough to easily wrap around the bulb and roots a couple of times.

3. Wrap the moss around the bulb tightly and then use florist's wire to wrap the moss several times in different directions, securing it tightly and neatly in place. Create a small loop of wire for hanging.

4. Mist your kokedama well or dunk it in water for half an hour. You can now position it in a tray or on a shelf alongside others, or pass fishing wire or cotton thread through the loop to hang it up.

EDIBLE INDOORS

There is no reason to limit your indoor plants to the purely ornamental. There are many plants that will grow happily indoors, look fantastic and contribute to beautiful and delicious meals into the bargain. Herbs can be grown very well in a bright kitchen or conservatory, sometimes producing pretty flowers and often possessing beautiful shapes, textures and scents, while little sprouting seeds of tasty plants can be developed on the tiniest tray. All bring life to a kitchen. With some imagination and a few excellent props, these indoor plants can look as good as they taste.

A WALL OF FLAVOURS

The kitchen shelves of cookery writer Debora Robertson are not just filled with stacks of plates, glasses and cake stands. All of these things are there and more, but nestled among them are herbs, cut flowers and scented pelargoniums, all jostling for space.

'I am in here a lot developing and testing recipes,' Debora says, 'so it is quite important that it is a good place to be. I spend a lot of time standing at the stove or the sink, both of which overlook the shelves. I look up and see a tableau of lovely things, and they change and evolve daily.' Debora works from home and feels that the plants she grows are essential not just to her cooking, but to creating a place that is conducive to work and play. 'Everyday beauty is important to me. We can't all have a Picasso in our kitchens, but we can have greenery, scent and flowers.'

Debora usually chooses edible plants such as scented pelargoniums, clove pinks and chillies, all of which end up in her cooking.

Debora and her husband Sean lived in the house for six years before they extended the galley kitchen. 'It meant that I knew exactly what my intention was by the time we did it,' she says, 'and I knew how I could create a lovely welcoming space. I wanted it exuberant and homely. I didn't want a clean, minimalist box, and I like it all being a bit over the top.' A large central island houses the sink, the hob and a large marble worktop that doubles as a place for diners. 'It is rather like having a bar in your kitchen,' she says. And then there are the shelves, lit from above by a huge skylight that runs the length of the side return extension. 'In summer it can get too hot in here for herbs so I put them outside, but in winter it is perfect.'

Debora grows many herbs that traditionally would live outside in the garden, and finds that those that would die down in the cold – mints and thyme, for instance – carry on producing new, fresh leaves all winter long if they are given a home indoors. Her favourite is lemon thyme. 'I use it in everything, sweet and savoury,' she says. 'If I am frying an onion I put in a few sprigs to add an extra layer of flavour, but I also love it used with apples and stone fruits.' Rather than grow easily available herbs such as parsley that are cheap to buy and used in quantity, she concentrates on those that are harder to find in the shops. Lemon verbena is her favourite of these, and she loves an infusion of its sherbet lemon-scented leaves for a refreshing afternoon tea. Clove pinks are present in her kitchen for their 'soft, old-fashioned, clovey scent', and she uses the petals in puddings or scattered into drinks, as she also does with her collection of scented pelargoniums.

A trip to Columbia Road Flower Market is a weekly fixture and helps Debora to keep her kitchen filled with flowers and plants.

The pinks and pelargoniums are topped up by Debora's weekly visits to Columbia Road Flower Market, where she buys flowers in abundance to fill her kitchen with colour and scent. She also acquires nearly all of her herbs there, from a family that has been selling herbs for three generations. 'They know that I am a bit of a magpie, and if they have anything unusual they call me over,' she says.

Above all, the kitchen with its wall of flavours is a place that enhances Debora's life. 'I love cooking and gardening and it is important to me to have plants here. I feel that the kitchen is personal, it reflects me. My wall of plants puts joy into my day.'

Sprouting seeds of flavourful herbs and other plants under glass domes create a kitchen display that is both beautiful and useful.

SPROUTING SUCCESS

'In London I can track down any herb I want', says Amanda Russell, 'but when I lived in north Yorkshire things were rather different. You grew the unusual stuff or you did without.' But in the capital city, Amanda has carried on her habit of growing a range of less well-known herbs, along with tasty seedlings for use in salads.

'I always have herbs here, but they are usually bought in. I pick up containers of basil and chives from the supermarket or garden centre and transfer them into white pots, partly because I like the look of them but also because giving them a little fresh compost sometimes keeps them going for longer.' And alongside them she grows small seedlings of other tasty plants. 'At the moment I have tiny seedlings of coriander and radish, and some pea shoots, and I have just started off some nigella seeds. I sow mustards in this way for sprouts, too, and carrots for carrot tops. They all make good and unusual additions to salads.' Amanda only does this over the winter, as the sun through her window gets too hot from around May onwards, so it is a way for her to have a constant stream of interesting and freshly grown flavours when the garden is at its bleakest. 'I love to see them growing,' she says. 'It makes me feel like spring is coming.'

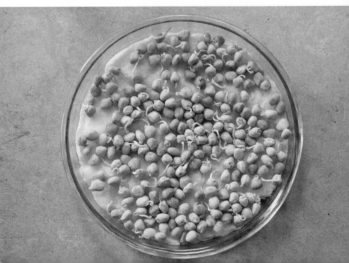

Amanda's method of growing these highly flavoured sprouts is 'very like the way we used to grow mustard and cress at school,' she says, adding, 'which I always found hysterically exciting.' Her vessels for her sprouts are about as far from old margarine tubs as you could imagine, though. 'I use beautiful old cake stands. Everyone has a few old cake stands, don't they? Well, I have a bit of a collecting habit and it seemed a good use for them.'

She also covers the seedlings with glass cloches and domes, which has the effect of framing and elevating them into something that looks far grander than posh mustard and cress. Once she has selected the cake stand she covers it with broken-up charcoal, which helps to reduce bacteria and prevents the whole set-up from becoming smelly. This is then covered with cotton wool, which can be moulded into shape once it is wet, and she sprinkles seeds thickly on top of that. She adds the dome to create a humid environment that will start off the seeds, but after three days removes the dome for a few hours each day to keep the inside fresh and to prevent moulds. The seeds usually take four or five days to germinate and the sprouts are ready to pluck and eat about ten days later. Amanda then discards the plants as they do not work well as 'cut and come again' crops when sown on cotton wool and indoors. 'You do have to sow quite thickly,' she says, 'so packets of seed from the garden centre are really a little too expensive for this particular method. Instead I find them from all sorts of different sources. I buy dried marrowfat peas for my pea shoots, coriander seeds from the Indian supermarket and cheap packets of herb and radish seed from the garden ranges of supermarkets. As these aren't going to become full-grown plants it doesn't matter what variety I buy.' She likes the opportunities this way of growing affords for experimentation. 'There is very little to lose in trying something new when you are growing like this. Why not give it a go?'

All kinds of seeds can be grown on cotton wool for use in salads or sprinkled onto dishes as a finishing touch, including nigella, chickpeas and garden peas. Amanda harvests them when they are 2.5cm (1in) or so tall.

Amanda grows useful kitchen herbs such as basil, mint and chives alongside her herb sprouts, planting each of them in pure white bowls and containers so that they look beautiful alongside the glass domes.

HOW TO:
REINVIGORATE MINT

Mint grown outside dies down in winter, but if you treat it as a houseplant over the winter months you will have a constant supply of leaves. As plants age they need a little attention, however, and there is a neat trick to keeping them youthful and vigorous.

1. Patches of mint slowly die off in the centre, their new shoots moving towards the edges of the clump. In a pot this means that the whole plant slowly loses its vigour.

2. Slip the plant out of its pot, take a serrated knife and saw straight down through the middle. Don't worry about harming the plant: mint is nearly impossible to kill, and all of the new growth will be around the edges anyway.

3. Bend one piece back on itself then slip it back into the pot so that the piece that was previously in the centre is now along the edge. Do the same with the other piece, pushing it into the pot so that the pieces are back to back.

4. Sprinkle on a little compost to fill any gaps and water this in to settle it. Alternatively, you can simply saw a mint plant into several pieces and make new plants in a series of smaller pots.

*Between them, Chelo Chile-Olmos
and Ollie Hudson keep the restaurant
at The Pig alive with an ever-changing
display of edible plants.*

TABLEFARE

**The restaurant at The Pig near Bath is filled with pots of herbs and
vegetables; they line every windowsill and are in the centre of every
table. 'We are aiming for a "Mr McGregor" feel,' says Ollie Hudson,
senior kitchen gardener for the hotel group. 'We want it to look like
an old-fashioned Victorian greenhouse, full of traditional terracotta
pots and plants.'**

The one rule on plants in the restaurant at The Pig is that they must be
edible, which is very much in line with the hotel and restaurant's ethos:
the kitchen garden lies just outside and guests can wander out and see the
vegetables that go into their meals. 'We aren't self-sufficient in vegetables
and fruit – we grow a little of everything we use and we source the rest
from within 25 miles (40km) of the hotel. But the chefs have a rule that
every plate must have been touched by the kitchen garden,' says Ollie.
And while the guests are eating from those plates, a small but choice
selection of some of the herbs grown by the gardeners is always within
reach. 'If guests pick a little bit off the plant on their table and sniff it or
nibble it, that's brilliant.'

Chelo creates interesting trays full of herbs and other edibles to place all around the restaurant. Every plant is different and all are beautifully grown.

Chelo Chile-Olmos is one of the gardeners at The Pig and the plants in the restaurant are her responsibility. The high quality of the display is no accident. 'I want to have beautiful and interesting edible plants on every table,' she says. 'But herbs and vegetable plants start to suffer if they are indoors for too long, so I have to change them around often.' Every Friday morning, between the end of breakfast at 10.30am and the start of lunch at 12.30pm, Chelo removes all of the plants on the 24 tables and those in six large trays positioned around the restaurant and replaces them with fresh ones – more than 150 plants going out and in. She checks the larger plants along the windowsills and changes any that are looking tired, then swaps those that are in darker parts of the restaurant with those in the conservatory area. The plants that go out are taken to the polytunnel, where they have a water, a feed and a rest, and may be repotted into fresh compost.

Chelo changes all of the plants every week and then pops in daily to check them. If anything is starting to look tired it is quickly replaced.

The gardeners use leftover plants from the walled garden but also seek out special cultivars especially for the restaurant, such as miniature tomatoes.

The indoor dining rooms are also filled with edible plants, humble turnips and strawberries rubbing shoulders with grand fireplaces and chandeliers.

In the polytunnel Chelo keeps at least 300 plants waiting in the wings and constantly sows and sources others. 'When we have finished planting out into the kitchen garden I say, "I'll take whatever is left!" and then I pot up the leftover beetroot plants, turnips, mustards, herbs and so forth.' She has a collection of more unusual herbs from which she constantly propagates new stock. 'I don't usually just put out the basil plants everyone can buy in a supermarket, I like to use lime basil, purple basil, 'African Blue' and 'Mrs Burns' Lemon'. It is more original to display herbs that guests have not come across before. They are always interested.' Chelo pots everything into antique terracotta pots and old wine crates. 'We use new terracotta in the garden, but that is not beautiful enough for the restaurant.'

She does not like to use a large number of flowers. 'I don't want guests to walk into what looks like a flower shop. The plants here are supposed to be edible, useful.' The few flowering plants that do grow here, such as geraniums, are also edible and she snips off the flowers and takes them to the chefs. 'I mainly want greenery. Mustard and legume flowers are allowed – they look just right, because they belong among the vegetable plants and herbs here. Guests love it that they can see the plants that will also be in the kitchen and on their plates.'

The styling of part of the restaurant is based around a Victorian greenhouse or potting shed.

BIG AND GREEN

The big green tropical plants are the stalwarts and the stars of the indoor garden world, filling a corner lushly, dominating a bay window, casting a jungly atmosphere over whole rooms. Big green plants have waxed and waned in fashion terms, though it is hard to imagine why they have ever lost their popularity. They do need some care and will look sorry for themselves if not given it, but with a little love they are glossy and beautiful. Their presence is always welcome and it is hard to picture a room that they would not improve. Cluster them together in one jungle-like gang, or place them here and there alongside beautiful pieces of furniture or art: wherever a big and green plant is put it will look fabulous.

The huge windows in Rob Stacewicz's London flat have allowed his collection of big, jungly houseplants to thrive.

WELCOME TO THE JUNGLE

Rob Stacewicz's front room is reminiscent of some remote colonial outpost. Huge, elegant palms dominate the room, combined with colourful, jungle-themed ornaments, beautifully intricate windows and a sweep of white curtains to give an effect that is more Malay bungalow porch than south London sitting room. A happy little pair of spectacled parrotlets in a large aviary complete the scene: a cool sundowner surely can't be far away.

Jungle-themed ornaments perch alongside an aviary containing two parrotlets, which look perfectly at home among all the verdant foliage.

Dramatic and spiky shapes dominate Rob's plant-filled room, as does the colour green, interspersed with splashes of vibrant colour.

Rob has cared for many of the plants for a great number of years, and several of them have grown to triffid-like proportions.

A tray of succulent plants is tucked into a corner, and Rob also grows seedlings under a set of horticultural lights.

Rob has travelled several times to tropical parts of the world such as Singapore for holidays and he loves the jungly look, but says he has re-created it in his own home almost by accident. 'I love my houseplants and have had some of them for a really long time, so I knew I needed to find a flat with lots of light. I chose this one mainly because it had huge windows, so they would be happy.' An enormous *Philodendron xanadu* is one of his biggest, acquired as a tiny cutting seven years ago. He thinks these plants are not for the average home, though. 'They just get too big, but you do get that almost instant retro Seventies look that big green houseplants bring. The philodendron now produces a new leaf every week, and they are getting bigger and bigger.' However, he does recommend it as a fantastic choice if you have the space: 'When the leaf is unfurling it looks completely alien.' Rob studied horticulture and clearly knows how to keep these plants happy, but they are particularly greedy and thirsty, and he needs to keep his constantly watered and fed. 'I can't mess around with one of those little houseplant watering cans: it needs gallons.'

Some of his plants are even older, and have been passed on to him by similarly green-fingered family members. 'I have two palms, *Chamaedorea elegans*, which are about 25 years old,' he says. 'My grandad passed them on to me. These palms are quite often grown as small houseplants but it is really unusual to see them with a trunk. In fact they are now both flowering and I am hoping that I have a male and a female. It would be great to get seeds.' An aspidistra is similarly venerable. 'They are extremely tough and here in London I could leave this out all year round. The leaves might get a bit ragged but it would survive.' Until recently Rob ran his own plant shop nearby, and several of his plants have come from there. Likewise, his parrotlets – Basil and Sybil – once lived in the shop, but look quite at home here among the greenery.

A couple of the palms (opposite) and a huge aspidistra are extremely old and were passed on to Rob by his grandfather.

Rob's tropical leanings are not confined to his sitting room and in early spring he uses a little indoor propagating unit and lights to start some interesting tender and exotic seedlings that will take his tropical look beyond the beautiful windows: daturas with their trumpet-shaped flowers, the brightly flowered annual climber *Ipomoea lobata*, commonly known as Spanish flag, and colourful pea-flowered *Sesbania* seedlings. All are kept happy under the bright lights and Rob's care until they can be planted outside. In fact, when Rob was studying it was annuals and native plants that most interested him, but he has found he loves the indoor plants more and more. 'I just really like being around plants and of course indoor plants extend the season. Sometimes winter can be six months long, or not far off that. It's nice to be able to potter around with plants at any time of year.'

A PLANT FOR EVERY PLACE

Nik Southern is the owner of London plant shop Grace & Thorn, but her days of living above the shop are behind her. 'I was right there for a while, when the business was starting up, but I have always loved the countryside. I grew up in Islington but when I was 19 I moved out to Essex – everyone else goes the other way!'

While Nik has had spells back in London, she has finally succumbed to the siren call of green fields and room to swing a cat – or rather three dogs, which pad contentedly around the house and garden. The light and space here have allowed her to fully indulge the love of houseplants that began in her childhood. 'My grandparents had a lot of houseplants – huge cheese plants, loads of geraniums. They had a bar in the living room, too, and all sorts of antiques. Their house was mental, but I loved it.' They inspired and nurtured her natural love of plants. 'I was the kid who was outside pruning forsythia while everyone else was off playing,' she says.

Plant-shop owner Nik Southern is an evangelist for the joy that houseplants bring and she has filled her own house with them.

Nik believes that houseplants can and should be fitted into every home, no matter how small. 'People think they don't have the space, but you can always fit in a houseplant, hanging from the ceiling or balanced on the windowsill,' she says. And while she has employed both of these methods to fit plants into her own home, she has also been able to really indulge her passion and fill it with huge and beautiful specimens that her London-based customers might really struggle to fit in. 'Many of these are refugees from the shop,' she says: if they catch her eye and don't quickly sell, they often find their way out to Essex.

Nik believes that every house, no matter how small, can contain houseplants, and her own home is an example of the many ways to use them. As well as more traditional houseplants she loves avocado seedlings and starts her own at home on a windowsill.

All of Nik's plants are in beautiful, shining condition, and she believes that everyone can take care of houseplants to similar standards; they just need to get to know their plants a little. 'It's so simple, but you do have to watch them, and be aware of them. Touch the compost and if it is dry then give them some water. Dust the leaves so that light can get to them. Mist the leaves, too, and don't be afraid to trim off brown tips – they are just like split ends of hair and plants look so much better without them.' She has noticed that increasing numbers of people want to use beautiful big houseplants as part of weddings and events and so has taken on a space near her home in which to collect and grow big specimens for hiring out. 'They really need to be plants that are looking their best for that kind of thing. We have to make sure they are in perfect condition, but that's no problem.'

Nik has brought houseplants to hundreds of London homes through her plant and flower business, Grace & Thorn, but she still makes plenty of time to care for her own large and beautiful collection.

Nik's own plants live among an eclectic collection of modern and antique furniture – she has her grandparents' leanings in furniture as well as in houseplants – and the large ones are given ample space to show off their shapes and habits. She likes to group smaller plants together on sets of shelves or windowsills. 'I like a mixture of textures and colours and my favourite smaller plant is oxalis. It's so spiky and different.'

Although Nik is thrilled to be out of London and back in the country to get her 'fix of green', she still couldn't be without plants indoors. 'I find it so soothing having something growing around me. The plants bring the whole house to life.'

Although plants are everywhere in Nik's house, they are often given plenty of space so that their shapes can be enjoyed. She is a stickler for good pots and goes to great lengths to source new and beautiful ones.

GREENING THE RUINS

There can be few head gardeners who work in the gardens where they romped in their childhood, but Joseph Atkin does. 'I went to school a few miles away, and all the boys used to come over here and play among the crumbling walls,' he says.

Aberglasney House was nearly a ruin then, having been left empty to slowly fall into disrepair after the 1970s. Joseph left the area and went to study at Kew, returning as a student when the house was undergoing restoration, and then later – to his obvious delight – taking on the role of head gardener.

The Ninfarium is an unusual indoor garden in the ruins of the oldest part of the house, once the servants' dining room, kitchens and a courtyard, and now Grade II listed. Joseph says, 'I can't claim credit but I remember Graham Rankin, the previous head gardener, bringing me in here and asking me what I would do with it. I said, "Stick a roof on it." It seems we were thinking along the same lines.'

Graham had been inspired by a visit to Ninfa, an Italian garden planted among ruins, and he named this Welsh version from a combination of 'Ninfa' and 'atrium'. 'The idea is in keeping with recent thinking on house conservation,' says Joseph. 'If a house is crumbling you cap it, put a roof on it, keep out the elements and let it be, rather than trying to piece it back together.' A glass roof was put on and shallow borders were created.

Joseph Atkin is the head gardener at Aberglasney and so is in charge of filling the Ninfarium with greenery and flowers.

This old and crumbling part of the house has been 'capped' with a roof, partly to conserve it and partly to create this extraordinary environment for plants.

'The borders have to be shallow because of the underlying archaeology. This is at heart a conservation project and we are always aware of that.' Plants were introduced and the Ninfarium was born.

The Ninfarium is heated by a heat source pump, but only to about 10–12°C (50–54°F), equivalent to a cool conservatory. But in some ways this indoor garden has to be treated very differently to a conservatory: Joseph says, 'The walls are lime mortar and if they were splashed with water they would be damaged.'

The area is barely heated, but there is just enough warmth in here to allow plants such as hardy bananas to flower and set fruit.

Begonia solananthera *climbs the old walls and flowers for much of the year, producing a sweet scent.*

Visitors love to see dramatic and colourful plants such as the stag horn fern and orchids, which all do well in the frost-free but shady conditions of the Ninfarium.

Flowering and foliage plants clamber among the beautiful and picturesque ruins of the grand house's old kitchens and servants' quarters.

'We water very carefully, and we can never damp down the paths to reduce the temperature on hot days as it would make the air too humid.' Each plant is watered individually, since care for the building is paramount.

The plants come from specialist conservatory nurseries and botanic gardens. 'Visitors want colour, so we are gradually finding plants that flower well in cool, shady conservatory conditions, but it is tricky because the tropical understorey – which our conditions equate with – is generally green,' says Joseph. He recommends clivias, pleione orchids and *Impatiens niamniamensis*, and is also seeking out half-hardy shrubs such as purple-flowered *Strobilanthes anisophylla* and the beautiful Brazilian fuchsia *Justicia rizzinii*. He is particularly delighted with a begonia planted at the base of one of the walls. 'You used to see *Begonia solananthera* in every hanging basket in the 1980s. It was only on planting it here that we realised it has adventitious roots, like ivy, and it climbs the wall and covers it in these pretty scented flowers.' But Joseph is happy that green is the predominant colour here, just as it was when he scrambled among the ruins as a schoolboy. 'My aim is to make it fuller, more jungle-like. I want the plants to reach out across the path and touch you as you walk by.'

Laura Jackson loves big green indoor plants and little delicate ones alike and they all grow happily in her bright and airy apartment, each given space to spread out and look its best.

GREEN SCREEN

The loft apartment of television presenter Laura Jackson is perhaps the finest possible setting for some really big and generous plants – all wide-open space, bare white walls and huge windows through which the daylight floods.

It was her best friend, living in New York, who first encouraged her interest in plants: 'In America houseplants are a much bigger presence than they are in the UK. Every home you go to in New York is full of them.' So Laura would visit and come back inspired to fill her own space with plants. Her boyfriend is also a houseplant lover, and keenly welcomed the arrival of more plants in the apartment. Several of their bigger, older plants are his, some of them derived from his grandmother. 'And I have to admit that he looks after them all,' says Laura. 'He loves them.' London plant shop Grace & Thorn was brought in to do a 'green makeover' on the apartment when it was being photographed by *Elle* magazine, and many of the plants that were brought along that day have stayed, too.

Laura is a keen foodie and runs the popular Jackson & Levine supper club in the apartment with her friend and BBC Radio 1 DJ Alice Levine, and she feels that the plants help them to create the atmosphere that their guests love. 'Grace & Thorn often lend us more plants for the occasions,' she says. 'We sometimes do foraging suppers – fennel pollen on potatoes, pea flower crostini, lots of herbs – and then it is good to have the place looking as green as possible.'

This is such an open space that it can take big plants. 'Your eye is drawn up to the high ceilings, so the big plants look perfectly to scale,' Laura says. One side of the apartment is almost entirely windows that consist of textured glass because a railway line runs parallel, so there is privacy for everyday life but also huge amounts of light for the plants. Having found great success with houseplants in these blessed conditions, Laura and her boyfriend have hunted out as many as they could find. 'We look out for them on Gumtree and eBay and have even picked them up via Freecycle. Houseplants grow so slowly that if you want big ones they will need to be old, so we look for them second-hand. Companies moving to new offices can be a good source, as they often have big houseplants and can't be bothered to take them with them.'

Laura has placed a large umbrella plant next to a huge map of the UK and northern Europe and elsewhere combines her plants beautifully with her collection of 1960s furniture. An asparagus fern sits alongside her record player and a money plant and cactus keep each other company on a little 1960s table.

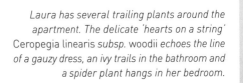

Laura has several trailing plants around the apartment. The delicate 'hearts on a string' Ceropegia linearis subsp. woodii *echoes the line of a gauzy dress, an ivy trails in the bathroom and a spider plant hangs in her bedroom.*

The apartment is not entirely dominated by the plants, however. Laura loves the style of the 1960s and the plants sit alongside furniture and art that she has collected from that period and beyond. Some of her more delicate and beautiful dresses, hung from the walls and alongside the plants, are pieces of art in themselves, even though the original motivation for hanging them was more practical than aesthetic: 'I just ran out of room in my wardrobe and I didn't want my more fragile dresses to be damaged, but now they are up on the walls I like them there.'

Laura's collection of plants may have begun almost by accident but she wouldn't do without them now, and they are tucked into every possible corner – hanging from the walls, nestling on windowsills and even trailing artfully in the bathroom. 'Having the plants has become really important to me. London can feel dusty and dirty but plants clean the air. They create a tranquil atmosphere here.'

HOW TO: LOOK AFTER LEAVES

Over time, leafy plants can become dull and dusty and develop brown tips. To keep them looking vibrant and alive, you need to give them a little regular care. The better condition you keep the leaves in, the more light will reach the plant and the better it will grow, so it is a virtuous circle.

1. The combination of houseplants and central heating is not a good one. Central heating dries the air, and this can lead to dulling of the leaves and browning of the tips. It is sensible to try to improve humidity levels around your plants by placing them on trays filled with pebbles and water. Mist them regularly, at least once a week in winter.

2. Even with regular misting, some plants will occasionally develop brown tips. There is no chance they will recover and green up, so go over the plant occasionally and snip them off. The plant will look better for it.

3. Wipe your glossy-leaved plants occasionally with a damp cloth to remove dust. Leaf-shine products may block the pores and prevent the plants from growing as strongly as they would otherwise, so just use lukewarm water and a soft cloth.

4. Plants with leaves that are hairy, textured or spiky cannot be washed, but still get dusty. Use a soft paintbrush to clean them occasionally.

Jack and Chris have filled their kitchen and its table with houseplants, the lightest and brightest area of the house and a place where they thrive.

HI-TECH HORTICULTURE

Jack Wallington loves his houseplants. 'I just really enjoy having them around me. I want to be surrounded by them. I grew up in the countryside and although I love living in London I do feel the need for that greenery.'

Jack is a keen gardener and has filled his little garden with dahlias and ferns, but this doesn't keep him going all year. 'In the winter many of my favourite garden plants die down; they are only fleeting. But my indoor garden looks good all year round.' His collection of plants is arranged on the kitchen table, sometimes to the chagrin of his partner, Chris Anderson. Plants are pushed back at mealtimes or moved if several people are coming for dinner. Both like to keep their home sleek and minimal – all is clean and white and there is not a bit of tat to be seen – but Jack's horticultural tendencies do slightly blur the sharp lines. 'The kitchen is where we spend a lot of our time, so I do like to have the plants in here,' says Jack. He is particularly keen on the little rabbit's foot ferns, *Davallia fejeensis*, which sit displaying their quirky fuzzy roots alongside the sleek cooker and slate-grey cupboard fronts.

96

Jack is a horticulture student and a keen gardener, and has developed a good set of green fingers.

Colourful foliage begonias, a pilea and a rabbit's foot fern (Davallia) are among the plants in the collection that is arranged around the couple's kitchen.

As well as wanting the plants near at hand, Jack chooses to keep his collection in the kitchen because it is so light. The couple recently had the room refurbished and they installed a large pair of French doors which open on to the garden and fold right back, allowing light to flood in. 'This is the brightest spot in the flat, so it makes sense to position the plants here,' says Jack, and they certainly look happy.

Despite his apparent lack of interest in the plants, Chris can take partial credit for their tip-top health. 'Chris uses my interest in plants as an excuse to get gadgets,' says Jack. Chris works for a technology company designing apps, and he has searched for ways in which he can help Jack to look after the plants using technology. One of his favourite gadgets is a weather station that is placed outside in the garden or indoors near the plants. 'It measures wind speed, temperature, moisture in the air, everything you need to know,' says Chris. 'We have one outside and one inside and all of this information is sent straight to my phone.' He has also bought a second gadget that works particularly well for indoor plants. 'It is a probe that I push into the soil and then program to let it know what the plant is. It will then tell me if the plant needs more water or light and what condition it is in – whether it is actively growing or dormant, for instance.' Jack agrees that these gadgets have been particularly helpful to him while he has been learning more about indoor plants: 'Without them you are just learning by killing the plants.'

Aeonium 'Zwartkop' and a foliage begonia enjoy the light that floods into the kitchen from two sides.

Jack has also been learning in a more traditional way by taking the RHS Level 1 and 2 courses, and is now studying the notoriously difficult RHS Level 3. 'I just wanted to know more about plants and it's great to get a really good grounding.' He clearly had green fingers before he started the course as his collection includes several plants that he has had for many years, including a large specimen of the 'ZZ plant', *Zamioculcas zamiifolia*, a Christmas cactus that was once his mother's and an aspidistra that belonged to his grandfather and has been through two world wars. Between them Jack and Chris have the know-how and the technology to keep their plants going for a lot longer yet.

The peace palm – a plant that particularly shows neglect – has glossy, well-cared-for foliage that suggests that the combination of Jack's gardening knowledge and Chris's technology are working.

THE COLLECTORS

For some indoor gardeners there is a higher purpose to their arrays of plants. These are the collectors, who have set themselves the task of bringing together a particular group of plants and growing them as well as they can. To start a collection is at heart a nerdy impulse, with half a mind to catalogues and text books, but it results in some of the most gorgeous displays, for when you know a plant intimately and understand all of its whims you can help it to grow at its best. There is a form of philanthropy at work here, too; some of the gardeners within this chapter are preserving their finds because the likelihood is that if they do not, these plants could vanish from cultivation. Their collections thrive under their expert care, and the results are beautiful.

The geodesic dome glasshouse provides the perfect conditions for Clive Groves' collection of violas: airy and not too hot nor too cold.

DOME-GROWN

'I have loved the smell of violets since I was a small boy,' says Clive Groves, who keeps a National Collection of Parma violets and sweet violets in a beautiful geodesic dome greenhouse in Devon. On a warm spring morning the scent inside the greenhouse is spectacular, the dome capturing and magnifying the perfume.

'For me the scent of violets brings back memories. This is a scent that used to be very common, but it is one we are losing today. When older ladies come in here they particularly recognise and love it,' Clive says. For him the scent is reminiscent of childhood days at his father's nursery, when the violets would be 'piled high'. In fact, he says, it is not just in the spring that the scent is good: 'The leaves of violets are also scented, and in fact are used to make violet oil – you need about 1 tonne of leaves to create 1kg (2¼lb) of oil. So it smells good in here even before the flowers are out. But of course the flowers have an even stronger and sweeter smell.'

Violets were originally grown around the big cities and were the third most popular cut flower in Britain, after roses and carnations, essential components of wedding bouquets. The scent has an anaesthetising effect on the nose, so posies were clutched close in the days when bad smells were ever-present in daily life. As urban industrial pollution increased, violet production moved to the West Country. 'Violets need clean air, and they particularly like the air that comes off the sea,' says Clive. Dorset, Devon and Somerset were the centre of production, and at the height of the trade Dawlish railway station shipped out 100,000 boxes of flowers a year. But then violets slowly fell out of fashion and nurseries began to close. 'My father heard that Winwood's violet nursery was shutting down and it looked as though their violet collection would be lost. So he bought it up and cared for it, and later I took up the mantle,' says Clive. He has the passion to keep on collecting and to breed new cultivars, several of which are named after family members. The latest is 'Amelia', a long-flowering 'quatre saisons' viola with a pinkish-purple flower held above glossy and puckered leaves, named after Clive's granddaughter.

Clive says that many people feel nostalgic about the smell of violas, and he wants to preserve them. Here (right) Viola *'Perle Rose' (far right),* V. *'Lady Hume Campbell', and (below)* V. *'Empress Augusta'.*

The geodesic dome – a half-sphere 4m (13ft) across and 2.7m (9ft) in height, made entirely out of triangles of glass – suits the violets' needs well. 'We grow two different types of violets,' says Clive. 'The sweet violets, *Viola odorata*, would be perfectly hardy left to grow outside all year round. We grow them in pots outdoors and then bring them in here to show them off while they are flowering. But the Parma violets need just a little bit of heat. We keep them at around 3°C (37°F) all winter. They are perfect plants for a very slightly heated greenhouse, conservatory or porch.' Violets are woodland plants that early in the year grow in light and bright conditions before the trees come into leaf, but they should not get too hot; the geodesic dome, which is excellent at regulating temperature, provides an ideal environment. Later on the violets need the shade of a woodland floor, so Clive moves them out of the dome and into a shade house for the summer.

It is important to Clive that he gets the conditions just right to allow the violets to thrive, as he has amassed a historically important collection which has now been formally recognised as a National Collection. He has since bought up collections that were in danger of being lost, and tracks down old cultivars from around the country and abroad. 'Many have been lost as their popularity has waned, and I think I have found most of those cultivars that exist in this country.' But Clive has found that the descendants of migrants to North America and Australia are a great source of older cultivars. 'Perhaps those gardeners who grew violets here didn't worry about keeping them going, as they knew there was a nursery down the road. But if you took a violet to Canada or New South Wales you looked after it or lost it, so they have been kept going for many years, and

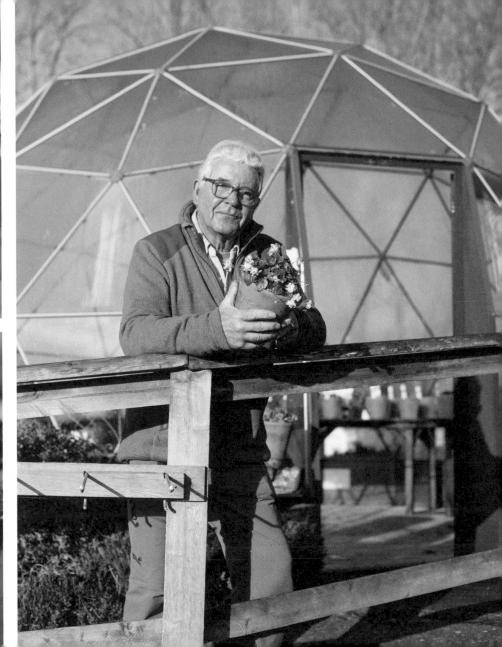

The lovely, pale-flowered
Viola 'Mrs R. Barton' in
its geodesic dome home.

families now realise they have something special. They get in touch because they realise that these plants are from England, and that they should be here.' Among these finds are 'Countess of Shaftesbury', a semi-double pink viola with a white-crested centre, bred by John Kettle of Corfe Mullen but tracked down in California, and 'Mrs Lloyd George', a semi-double purple flower bred in Dorset but in his collection via Australia.

'I am a violet freak,' says Clive. 'I think they are quite magical and the scent makes me go weak at the knees. They are wonderful plants and I want to do my best to preserve them.'

HOW TO: MULCH

Mulching is the practice of covering the surface of a plant's compost. This is worth doing for two reasons: it helps to seal in moisture and reduce the need for watering, and it looks nice. If you are going to use a mulch you will have to plant a little deeper into the pot and leave more space between the surface of the compost and the rim of the pot. Here are a few options for topping your containers.

1. Coconut fibre hanging-basket liner is a cheap, useful and easily available mulch and can be used under any houseplant to cover the compost.

2. Pine cones can be collected from woodland for free. They look good, add their own texture, and are particularly lovely under woodland plants such as ferns.

3. Gravel is a straightforward and very easy-to-find material to use as a mulch. It is particularly good at keeping the contents of a pot cool and moist.

4. You can also use creeping plants to cover the surface. Here *Ficus pumila* and *Pilea glaucophylla* nestle around a larger plant, entirely covering the compost.

One of many cymbidium hybrids that, along with an impressive collection of other orchids, fill Tom and Rose Price's conservatory with colour almost all year round (left). Cymbidiums and phalaenopsis provide bright yellows and pinks (opposite).

GLORIOUS ORCHIDS

Even on a chilly spring day, Tom and Rose Price's conservatory is filled with colour from cattleyas, dendrobiums, pleiones and phalaenopsis in deep pink, pale pink, yellow, red and white, and all shades in between.

'It's not at all unusual to have so much in flower,' says Rose. 'We are members of the Cheltenham and District Orchid Society, and with contributions from all of the members who have something to show we are able to do a table display each month. Every month of the year there is colour on it.' Tom and Rose have always loved gardening and tend a 0.8ha (2 acre) plot encompassing a mini arboretum, an orchard and herbaceous and shrub borders, but it was their daughter, helping a local orchid collector as part of her work experience, who first piqued their interest in orchids. 'She had been helping to pot up cymbidiums. She brought home a couple of backbulbs, and that was it,' says Tom. The couple now have two large greenhouses packed full of orchids, in addition to those that they display to such fabulous effect in their conservatory.

Miltoniopsis, *often known as the pansy orchid (left) and* Dendrobium nobile *(below).*

The conservatory is kept fairly cool, at 12°C (54°F), with a heater that kicks in when the temperature drops. 'We mainly have cool-growing orchids that have no great need for heat,' says Tom, 'so they are pretty easy in the cool conditions of a conservatory or a porch.' Phalaenopsis, the moth orchid, which has become such a popular houseplant, likes more heat and so is happier in the house than most, he adds. Just as important as the conservatory heater is a fan attached to the house wall that periodically kicks in to keep the air moving.

'Orchids are slow-growing,' says Tom, 'and that means that if you do anything wrong you will be looking at it for years.' He cites an incident when he decided to make up his own orchid fertiliser but made it too strong, so that it burnt the leaf tips of several of the orchids. 'I won't forget that in a hurry,' he says. He has an easy-to-remember formula for feeding orchids now: weekly, weakly. 'There is also the question of sun,' he says. 'You can grow them in lots of sun and get a few burnt tips but lots of flowers, or give them shade and get fewer flowers. I lean towards the few burnt tips.' He only gives them extra shading for a month either side of midsummer.

Tom holding a Dendrobium nobile *type orchid (far left, top); the unusual* Macodes, *known as the jewel orchid (far left, bottom); a pitcher plant,* Nepenthes coccinea, *one of the few non-orchidaceous plants in the Price's collection (left, top); and a phalaenopsis (left, bottom).*

All of this expertise has come about through years of contact with other orchid growers. 'I didn't know much about them, so I started helping out at the Orchid Society table at meetings and flower shows. I always found myself alongside someone who knew what they were talking about so I took it all in.' He now gives talks on orchid cultivation himself. But the fund of expertise is dwindling; the extent of the Prices' collection is partly down to the fact that fellow orchid-growers have died and specialist nurseries have closed down, and they have taken on parts of the collections. 'If people have been collectors for a while they are going to have some things that you might never see again.'

It is the enthusiasts such as Tom and Rose who are keeping the interest in these orchids alive and passing on the knowledge of how to care for them. But above all they have created a beautiful, rainbow-hued corner of their home, a place to sit and gaze at the flowers and drink a cup of tea all year round.

HOW TO: CARE
FOR ORCHIDS

ENCOURAGING A MOTH ORCHID TO FLOWER AGAIN

Phalaenopsis, known as the moth orchid, is one of the most commonly available orchids because it is happy in the warm, centrally heated conditions of most homes. This is how to encourage flowering once your initial flower spike has gone over.

REPOTTING A CYMBIDIUM

Excess leafless bulbs on an orchid can lead to a plant that is not vigorous and does not flower, so occasionally it is important to pull the plants out of their pots, clean and split them and repot in fresh compost.

1. When the flowers have faded, do not cut off the whole of the flower spike. Look along the spike and you will see a number of small pale green buds. Each of these has the potential to produce a new flowering spike. Cut the stem to just above the top bud and you should soon get a new flower. Once that is over cut back to the next bud, and so on, until all are gone.

2. As soon as you have cut the spike, dab the cut end with a little ground cinnamon. It is a natural fungicide and will help to prevent any rots from developing.

1. Tip the orchid from its pot. Orchid compost is very loosely packed, so it is important to do this over a bucket or tray.

2. Use a serrated knife to slice off the bottom half of the root ball. This will make it easier to tease out the shoots and will encourage new roots to form.

3. Pull the plant gently apart into small sections.

4. Fill the bottom of a new pot with orchid compost. This must be a loose, chunky mixture of bark, coir, hydroleca pellets and charcoal.

5. Pull away the old leafless bulbs to find the growing point. Cymbidiums grow sideways across the pot, so you need to find the growing point and then place the offshoot to one side of the pot so that it has space to grow.

6. Fill back in with fresh compost and then water well.

Matthew is the youngest-ever curator of the Royal Horticultural Society's garden at Wisley, and his love of plants can be seen in his home as well as his work.

THE BEST OF BOTH WORLDS

Matthew Pottage and his partner Kishan Athureliya are both collectors, though of very different things. Kishan loves interiors and has acquired an eclectic mix of 18th-century French furniture and Indian artefacts, while among these nestles Matthew's precious collection of unusual indoor plants.

'I have always loved houseplants,' Matthew says. 'My grandma had pelargoniums and cacti and I took an interest really early on.' A huge ponytail palm, *Beaucarnea recurvata*, is a testament to those early green-fingered years. 'I bought it as a tiny plant when I was a kid and just loved looking after it. Now it is vast.' And it is surrounded by other choice and beautifully tended plants. The two collections combine to make an unusual and opulent indoor garden.

But the ponytail palm is not particularly typical of his collection. 'I especially look out for plants with variegated and glaucous foliage – they really appeal to me,' Matthew says. And it is no surprise that he has access to an inspiring range of plants, for at 29, he is the youngest-ever curator of one of gardening's greatest institutions: Wisley, the flagship garden of the Royal Horticultural Society. Several of his houseplants have been acquired from the garden's shop, which often sells a greater range of plants than you would find in the average garden centre. 'I am a big fan of oddities. I love unusual foliage, and I have picked up things as I have gone around nurseries and gardens, and been given plants by friends.' His favourite is a variegated mother-in-law's tongue, *Sansevieria trifasciata* 'Bantel's Sensation', which he has had for about 15 years. It is very slow-growing, as are most variegated plants, because they do not contain the same levels of chlorophyll as all-green plants and it is chlorophyll that helps a plant to convert sunlight into growth. 'You cannot just place them in your sunniest spot to compensate, since on many of them the paler parts will burn in harsh sunlight,' says Matthew. Despite this he is still smitten. 'I love the contrast, and the way they light up a dull corner. If flowers didn't exist I would still love plants just for their foliage.'

In some places Matthew's and Kishan's interests have combined to excellent effect. Matthew has filled a series of urns picked up from flea markets with his plants, most spectacularly *Platycerium wandae* – a glaucous form of stag horn fern – in a rusted urn. He has also created three terrariums from extravagantly fluted glass jars. 'Kishan wanted some glass urns for the table and loved the shapes of these, so I filled them with plants that need high humidity.' *Nertera granadensis*, commonly known as the coral bead plant, *Adiantum capillus-veneris* (maidenhair fern) and a patch of moss were all chosen because they would curl up and die if they were not kept well watered and in a humid atmosphere.

Most extravagantly, Matthew has removed the innards from an antique chair and planted it up with pink-flowered *Medinilla magnifica*. 'I bought the chair at an antiques fair exactly for this purpose because it had such a deep seat. The stallholder told me that the springs needed replacing, and I think he was quite surprised when I said that I was going to remove them and turn it into a plant pot. I don't think Kishan was too sure at first, but I love it.' It seems the perfect way to display one of Matthew's more showy plants within this antiques-obsessed household.

A ponytail palm, a series of glass terrariums,
a bonsai pine and a medinilla planted into the seat
of a chair are among Matthew's eclectic collection.

Matthew's interest in plants and his partner Kishan's love of antiques combine in a series of dramatically shaped urns, planted with equally impressive species such as the stag horn fern.

TINY TREASURES

Indoor plants don't have to be big to make an impact. Some of the prettiest of plants are the tiniest: little succulents and cacti, ferns and trailing plants. Gather them together on a shelf, in a porch or on a windowsill and they become a collection of textures, shapes and tones, each made all the more lovely by its proximity to its companions and their contrasting foliage. The plants in this chapter may be small, but they are little gems, beautiful horticultural treasures, and they deserve to be gathered together and admired.

SUCCULENTS BY THE SEA

In the little porch that leads into the Whitstable home of garden writer Francine Raymond, succulent plants in many forms and colours jostle for space.

'In the past they seemed a bit of a guilty pleasure,' she says of them. 'They have only very recently become fashionable, so I was always slightly embarrassed about them. And yet I could never seem to help collecting more.' Succulents are so called because their stems and leaves are thick and full of water to allow them to survive in the dry climates in which they naturally grow. Along these little shelves Francine has echeverias in multiple shapes and shades, aeoniums, sempervivums, sedums and aloes. 'There are always more, each with a slightly different shape or colour. And because they are so easy to propagate everyone has a go, so you can find them at flea markets and jumble sales – there is no need to visit a nursery or even a garden centre. They are incredibly easy to come by, and I can't resist.'

Francine's sunny seaside porch is unheated but stays frost-free and is the perfect spot for her collection of succulents.

The plants are displayed upon finds from local flea markets, such as a tiny old chest of drawers and a set of wirework shelves. Many of the containers are flea market finds too.

Francine grows a great number of echeverias, which come in many leaf shapes and shades of pale silver blue.

Francine's succulents are the remnants of a larger collection of plants that lived in the conservatory of a previous house. 'I had all sorts of houseplants in there, but conservatories are dangerous places: too hot in summer, too cold in winter, and too easily ignored when they are not comfortable to be in. These plants are the last ones standing, the only survivors.' The porch is unheated, and sometimes gets very hot, sometimes cold – though never down to freezing, no doubt partly because of the house's proximity to the sea. 'These succulents generally come from deserts where it gets very hot in the day and very cold at night. They store the water they need,' says Francine. 'Indoors would be too hot for them, but outdoors they would get wet in the rain and rot off, so this is the perfect spot. One of the things I don't like about houseplants is that they are so dependent on you, but these are very easy, particularly out here. They need a little watering but not much, and once a year I take them out of their pots, tidy them up and repot them. That's all they ask.'

Nearly all of the plants live in terracotta pots. 'I think they look beautiful in terracotta, and they are happiest in them too.' They need very good drainage and will rot if planted into a normal multipurpose compost, so Francine uses a half-and-half mixture of horticultural grit and peat-free multipurpose. She waters the plants once a week during the growing season and gives them an occasional feed. In return for this fairly minimal effort she has a beautifully textured collection of succulents in myriad shapes and forms, and mostly in shades of silver and grey that tone in beautifully with the slate grey colour of the porch's woodwork.

This woodwork has to be repainted every year because the sea air and high light levels in Whitstable cause it to fade, but it is a colour that Francine loves and uses again and again throughout her house. She has arranged the plants in the porch on finds from flea markets – several little wirework shelves hung against the side windows and leaning against the walls, a small chest of drawers – and in among the bits and pieces of family life such as umbrellas and the fossils collected by her son when he was younger. All together they make for the perfect seaside porch of useful and interesting things and indoor plants that can very nearly look after themselves.

Francine finds succulents extremely easy to propagate, and she is not the only one. She has amassed her collection from finds at jumble sales and extras from friends. Her porch provides the perfect spot to admire them, along with her son's collection of fossils.

HOW TO: TAKE CUTTINGS OF SUCCULENTS

Succulents are among the houseplants that are very simple to propagate yourself. You can easily bulk up your numbers and create new plants to sell or to give away to friends.

1. Take your cutting. Tiny succulent plants can be created from a single succulent leaf if material is scarce, but this is a slow – if magical – way of going about it. Instead, take whole shoots if you can.

2. Leave your cuttings to sit for a couple of days. There is so much moisture in the stem that they can rot off if put straight into compost after cutting. After two days the cut surface will have callused over, and this is the time to move on to the next stage.

3. Using a mix of about 50:50 compost and grit, fill small pots and push a hole in the centre of them. Insert your cutting and settle the compost around it.

4. Spread grit over the surface, then water well.

PLANT-MINDED PEOPLE

The walls of Grace & Thorn, a florist and plant shop in East London, are lined with chunky, industrial concrete shelves and packed full of plants. 'During the week we sell mainly flowers,' says florist Evelina Favaro, who has worked in the shop for just over a year, training in floristry on the job, 'but at weekends it is all plants, nothing but plants.'

On Saturday shoppers from Broadway Market come along and on Sundays the shop attracts the stragglers from Columbia Road Flower Market. This is a perfect spot for catching plant-minded people in a buying mood. The shop has also nurtured a set of devotees via its stylish and inclusive presence on Instagram, on which followers are encouraged to post their own houseplant pictures with the hashtag #greenupyourgaff. 'The Instagram followers come in at the weekend and they are always delighted to see it for real. They take their own pictures. To them it is like visiting a museum,' says Evelina.

All of the plants in Grace & Thorn are arranged to give space-pressed Londoners ideas on how to use them in their homes – every container is small, beautiful and quirky.

Owner Nik Southern started the shop because she felt that there was a gap in the market. 'I hate the way garden centres display houseplants. My idea was to show people how you can use them in your home, how great they can look.' The shop has a 'no brown pots' rule. When plants come in they are almost instantly distributed into an array of beautiful and unusual pots that Nik sources from across Europe, and Denmark and Belgium in particular: concrete cast pots, sleek copper pots, geometrically shaped pots, and many more. 'I am completely obsessed with finding new pots. I go to Europe at least once a year to track down new pots and new suppliers. I want to have pots that no one else offers. We also commission three local artists to make them for us. It is important to me that we are showing people how to display their plants in the most gorgeous way.'

Also on sale are many plant hangers, and there's a hanging plant installation service as well as macramé hanging basket-making nights. 'People don't have the tools or the skills to do such things themselves, so we try to make it all easy.' Nik is considering a 'repotting night', where locals can bring along their pot plants, buy pots and get a boost of confidence from the experts. In essence, she is doing whatever it takes to encourage those living in little London flats to fill their homes with plants, no matter how small and discouraging their space. 'Lots of people around here are tenants and plants are an inexpensive way to make a change in your home, even if your home is only temporary. People tell me they have no room, but you can always hang a plant, or fit plants along a mantelpiece or shelf.'

Evelina herself has completely fallen for the plants since she started working in the shop. 'My flat is full of houseplants now,' she says. She loves 'anything with heart-shaped leaves' and in particular trailing philodendron and the colourful foliage begonias. 'It is important that we grow plants ourselves because people come in and they are not confident. They want to know exactly how to grow the plants. If you have grown them yourself you can advise them better.' The near-constant trail of houseplant-hungry customers suggests that locals are gaining in green-fingered confidence, and that more and more of East London's rented flats are filling up with greenery – and beautiful pots.

Animal-head pots are among Grace & Thorn's most popular items. 'They make wonderful presents,' says Evelina, 'especially when planted up with something small, and they will fit onto anyone's windowsill.'

Sandy loves the geometric shapes of the cacti and succulents and thinks they have an 'alien' look.

COOL CACTI

'I get a bit overwhelmed by colour,' says Sandy Burnfield, 'so I don't particularly like flowers in the house. But these plants are different.' He is talking about the collection of cacti and succulents he and his wife Penny have accumulated, which lives outside in the summer and divides its time in the winter between a cool greenhouse and the house.

Sandy loves the strange shapes and architectural structure. 'There's an alien oddness to them; they have real character, much more so than any flower.' Penny, who maintains the couple's beautiful garden filled with flowers, fruit and vegetables and opens it regularly to the public, clearly doesn't hold quite the same grudge against flowers, but she is very happy to have these beautiful plants up close where she can enjoy them. 'We bring them into the house when something is flowering or just looking particularly good,' she says. 'In summer we put them on the tables so that our visitors can appreciate them up close while they are enjoying their tea and cake, but in the winter this display is for ourselves.' This is when they line the shelves of their sunniest windowsills with weird and wonderful cacti and succulents.

One of Sandy's favourites is the cobweb houseleek (bottom left) because of its beautiful and unusual texture.

The plants, including Aeonium 'Zwartkop' (below left), will only do well indoors in winter for short spells, after which Penny moves them back out to a cool but frost-free greenhouse.

Although the collection was originally started by Sandy, health problems have meant he has had to hand over its care to Penny. She grows the plants in a frost-free greenhouse for much of the winter, in plenty of light, and just brings them indoors for relatively short spells. 'In the summer they are outside and I water and feed them freely,' she says. 'But in winter in the greenhouse they don't need much at all. When I bring them into the house it is a different matter – the warmth means that they need a little bit more care, and the odd trickle of water.' Each will spend a couple of weeks indoors and then be moved back out to the greenhouse to recover, their place in the house taken by another, fresher plant. 'They don't need much care apart from that,' says Penny. 'I repot them once a year, partly because they can become difficult to water when they have filled their pots. I pick them over in winter for any dead bits. I always use gloves with the spikier ones.'

The couple have several aeoniums picked up on travels to Tresco, Isles of Scilly, including nearly black-leaved 'Zwartkop', green and glossy-leaved *Aeonium haworthii*, and the flat disk of *A. tabuliforme*. 'In Tresco they grow everywhere – the conditions are so perfect for them,' says Penny. 'They appear in cracks in walls and in tree trunks. Here we have to try a little harder with them.' Mainly this means providing a terracotta pot with a single crock over the drainage hole and a well-drained, gritty soil, giving them lots of light, keeping them frost-free in the winter, and being very patient. 'They do change, but they change very slowly,' says Penny. 'Every now and then one of them surprises you by suddenly producing flowers.'

One of Sandy's favourites is a *Sempervivum arachnoideum*, the cobweb houseleek, a series of tight little rosettes covered in fluffy fibres here packed into a beautiful, squat terracotta pot. 'They are just so easy on the eye,' says Sandy. 'I don't even look at a daffodil for very long because the bright yellow bothers me. Flowers can be hard work for me: give me one of these weird and wonderful, alien foliage plants any day.'

Penny has taken over the care of the collection in recent years, watering and feeding them relatively freely during the summer when they are outside, but less often when they are in the greenhouse during the winter.

147

HOW TO:
POT ON CACTI

Cacti and succulents grow very slowly, but it is still a good idea to pot them on into slightly bigger pots each spring. As they fill their pots they become more difficult to water and although they don't need a huge amount, restricting it too much will slow their growth even further.

1. Create a compost for a cacti or a succulent by creating a 50:50 mix of multipurpose compost and horticultural grit.

2. Tip the plant carefully out of its old pot and allow some of the grit and compost to fall away from it.

3. Repot it in a slightly larger pot, placing a crock and 2.5–5cm (1–2in) of the compost mix at the bottom of the pot first. Fill in with the mix all around the sides and push in to firm it around the roots.

4. Finally, top with a layer of grit to keep moisture away from the surface.

A GREEN CORNER

Katie Wallis's indoor garden is a tiny, sunny nook off one corner of her kitchen. 'It could so easily have just been a place we passed through from the kitchen to the front room,' she says, 'but it has become a special quiet spot. My son sits here to read, I sit here to sew.'

Katie also enjoys tending the plants that are arrayed along the shelf above her sofa and on the table by her French doors. 'They are mainly hand-me-downs from friends and relations. Some are from my mum. All of the cacti belonged to an Australian friend who lived nearby. When he decided to move home he couldn't take them with him, so he passed them on to me. I love their spiky shapes and they love it here.'

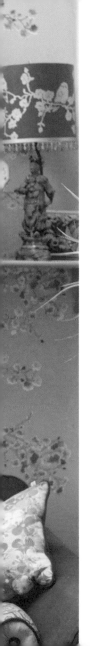

The conservatory is squeezed into a former side return, making a beautiful, plant-filled nook for Katie and her family to relax in.

A purple oxalis sits on a mosaic table top that was created by Katie.

All plants here have to be able to thrive in hot and dry conditions and the cacti and succulents do particularly well, needing very little care.

When Katie and her husband Simon first moved into the house, this corner was a ramshackle lean-to conservatory with a small brick wall facing onto the garden. They had it rebuilt with a wooden frame and French doors. A sturdy shelf was put up on which to arrange houseplants, and a comfy sofa was moved in. As gorgeous as they are, the plants here are slightly upstaged by the fabulous stencilled wall behind them. Both Katie and Simon are artists and while Katie works mainly in textiles and screen printing, she has also dabbled in stencils and wall coverings. 'My brother bought a château in France and was doing it up. He saw some wallpaper he loved that had a beautiful cherry blossom pattern on it, but as it cost £120 per roll he asked me if I could do something similar. I made a stencil and painted his wall. I have used the same stencil in a couple of different places now, but this is my most successful colourway.' The jade green she has used is a beautiful foil for the plants. Katie also specialises in making lampshades, one of which sits alongside the plants, and the cushions and sofa throw are also her own work. Much of the work throughout her house centres on bees, often used to create patterns within honeycombs or geometric grids or flowers, but, she says, 'I am moving on to bats now, and then I think hummingbirds. I have a thing for pollinators.'

One of the few flowering plants in the reading nook is a jasmine, bought for a hanging basket, but she is planning to replace it with a 'string of pearls' succulent (*Senecio rowleyanus*) as the jasmine is struggling with the conditions here. The drought-loving cacti fare particularly well because it can become a hot environment. 'In the summer the sun shines right in from about 11am. It gets really warm, particularly when the French windows are closed. So it is only plants that can cope with that blast of heat that do well here.' Her husband Simon is a keen allotment grower and also finds this a fantastic space for sowing and growing plants for his plot. 'He has just potted up his tomatoes and he grows them on the tabletop by the doors until it is time to plant them out. The light is good, so they do well.' The tabletop is another of Katie's projects, this time a mosaic in keeping with the mosaic on her kitchen walls, itself 'an ode to Tottenham Court Road tube station', a reference to the Eduardo Paolozzi mosaic, part of which was removed during a redevelopment. Katie and Simon's house is filled with art, and this little reading, sewing and growing corner is no exception.

SOURCES

PLANT SOURCES

London Terrariums
londonterrariums.com

Grace & Thorn
graceandthorn.com

Groves Nurseries
grovesnurseries.co.uk

OTHER CONTRIBUTORS

Cheltenham and District Orchid Society
cheltenhamorchids.org

Emma Bradshaw's blog, Bradshaw & Sons
emmabradshaw.blogspot.co.uk

Amanda Russell
randbdesigns.co.uk

The Pig at Bath
thepighotel.com

Aberglasney House and Gardens (Ninfarium)
aberglasney.org

Francine Raymond's website and blog
kitchen-garden-hens.co.uk

Find Penny and Sandy Burnfield's garden 'Terstan',
which opens for charity, on the National Gardens
Scheme website
ngs.org.uk

Katie Wallis's textiles and designs
katiewallisprint.com

AUTHORS

Photograph by Kirstie Young

Photograph by Jason Ingram

WORDS BY LIA LEENDERTZ

Lia Leendertz writes regular gardening columns for *The Telegraph* and *The Garden* magazine and is a frequent contributor to several other gardening magazines and to *The Guardian*. She studied horticulture at the Royal Botanic Garden, Edinburgh, and has won several awards for her writing. She lives with her family in Bristol and has a town garden, an allotment and a burgeoning collection of houseplants. Lia is the author of *My Cool Allotment* and *My Tiny Veg Plot*, also published by Pavilion.

LIA'S ACKNOWLEDGEMENTS

I would like to thank all of the wonderful contributors to this book for opening up their homes and giving us their time and expertise. It is such a treat to be able to write a book in this way, based on the experience of so many interesting and knowledgeable gardeners. I have learnt a huge amount and met some wonderful people along the way.

Thanks to Mark Diacono for his brilliant skills with a spreadsheet and an itinerary. The photos aren't at all bad, either!

Finally, thank you to all at Pavilion who steered this book to completion, in particular Krissy for ever-cheery management, but also to Polly, Katie, Diana, Laura and Claire. Thanks, Lia

PHOTOGRAPHY BY MARK DIACONO

Mark runs Otter Farm, a unique smallholding in Devon where he grows everything from peas to pecans. When he's not running courses and events at Otter Farm, he's writing and photographing either his own books or other people's.

MARK'S DEDICATION

For my family